Wicca For Beginners:

The Book of Spells and Rituals for Beginners to Learn Everything from A to Z. Witchcraft, Magic, Beliefs, History and Spells

Table of Contents

Chapter 1: **Historical Foundation Of Wicca**..5

Chapter 2: **Wiccan Rede And Ardanes**..13

Chapter 3: The Divinity Of Wicca..................62

Chapter 4: Your Start With Wicca.................70

Chapter 5: Spellwork.......................................79

Conclusion..92

© **Copyright by Judith Guise 2019 - All rights reserved.**

The content contained within this book may not be reproduced, duplicated or transmitted without direct written permission from the author or the publisher.

Under no circumstances will any blame or legal responsibility be held against the publisher, or author, for any damages, reparation, or monetary loss due to the information contained within this book, either directly or indirectly.

Legal Notice:

This book is copyright protected. It is only for personal use. You cannot amend, distribute, sell, use, quote or paraphrase any part, or the content within this book, without the consent of the author or publisher.

Disclaimer Notice:

Please note the information contained within this document is for educational and entertainment purposes only. All effort has been executed to present accurate, up to date, reliable, complete information. No warranties of any kind are declared or implied. Readers acknowledge that the author is not engaging in the rendering of legal, financial, medical or professional advice. The content within this book has been derived from various sources. Please consult a licensed professional before attempting any techniques outlined in this book.

By reading this document, the reader agrees that under no circumstances is the author responsible for any losses, direct or indirect, that are incurred as a result of the use of information contained within this document, including, but not limited to, errors, omissions, or inaccuracies.

Chapter 1: The Historical Foundation of Wicca

For a beginner, it's important to understand the ideology behind what you're about to engage in, so for that this chapter will be your stepping stone. In it, you will learn basic definitions as well as the in depth history of the founding craft members that made Wicca what it is today. So let's start with some definitions.

Basic Definitions.
Wicca - a neopagan practice created in the mid-twentieth century. It has pre-Christian roots and is considered an Earth-based craft. This is a polytheistic faith with many writings discussing etiquette, customary practices, sabbats, ceremonies, the divinity, and lastly magicks. The doctrine one would consider for Wicca is called a Rede. While it is not as strict or binding as Christians are with the bible, this is a very important manifest in witch decorum.

Coven - usually consisting of 10 to 15 members who were initiated into the ranks. Covens normally have their own set of practices based on a variation, interpretation, or an aspect of the Wicca faith. As a member of said coven, you are in understanding those practices and interpretation. Ranks are labeled with degrees of order, such as first degree for mastery of magic, second degree for mastery of ceremonies, and the third degree for those who wish to enter into the priestesshood. The priestess degrees have their own marks of mastery. Each mark of mastery comes as a result of tutelage from the coven's leader.

Paganism - generally accepted as any form of religious practice outside of mainstream religions like Christianity, Judaism, and Islam; though this term is normally used in regards to non-Christian or biblical practices. The term was first found to be used in the fourth century by early Christians to describe people within the Roman Empire who continued to have polytheistic practices.

Neopaganism - is regarded as a contemporary version of practicing historical pagan traditions, away from conventional religious practices. However, today's neopagan is not bound to not practice any mainstream religion if they so believe this is their way. This contemporary movement is an open and accepting form of faith where the individual can have a mix of traditional and mainstream faiths if they so, please.

The Foundation Of The Wiccan History.
Gerald Gardner (1884 - 1964), also known as the "Father of Wicca," is responsible for the modern world's definition and practice of witchcraft and founded Gardnerian Witchcraft back in the mid-twentieth century after the repeal of the Great Britain Witchcraft Acts in 1951. He utilized his varied knowledge of his career stay and observations in Asia, his knowledge as a Free Mason, his time practicing the craft with other covens, his inspiration from the Margaret Murray essay on the Witch-

Cult Hypothesis, as well as the writings from the British mysticism occultist Edward Alexander Crowley (infamously known as Aleister Crowley) to make this possible. Through his Brick Wood Coven, Gardner was able to initiate many, including those who would pass their mark of mastery into High Priestesshood. These masters, in turn, would go on to either make their own covens or join a new one. Gardner himself stated that the term "Wica" was referred to him from witches he initially met as a way to describe themselves while the phrase "Witch Cult" was to describe their religion. Wica was later turned into Wicca as later publications began to standardize it's spelling, though it is said that a man named Charles Cardell was the first to coin the term. However, even his reference goes back to his mother's use of "Wiccen." A museum is dedicated to Gerald Gardner's work. The Museum of Witchcraft is on the Isle of Man and is open to the public for the world to view his, and his companions', works in making Wicca publicly accepted as a nature-based faith by providing further education on the craft instead of keeping it a deep dark secret with heinously dark intentions.

Along with Gardner, Wicca would not be where it is now without the immense influence of Doreen Edith Dominy Valiente (1922 - 1999) who wrote many research papers, books, and broke ground on new Wicca traditions. Doreen is also known as the Mother of Modern Witchcraft for her contributions towards the refinement of the Wicca craft. It was her iconic eight words that came to be known as the Wiccan Rede. It was Doreen's practical knowledge of magic as a teenager and her extensive research into the various types of craft, as well as the knowledge she possessed as a High Priestess that, not only headed her towards forming her own coven but as an influential member of other covens too.

She wrote much of the early customs, ethics, decorum, and etiquette of Wicca while in the Gardnerian era Brick Wood coven during its founding years. Gerald Gardner initiated Valiente himself as the coven's High Priestess. She later parted ways with the coven due to directional differences in law, new tradition, coven customs, and Gardner's own behavior towards the publicity and acceptance of Wicca. Doreen was instrumental in breaking the mold on initiation rules dictating that one can only be initiated into a coven by a pre-existing member. She advocated for anyone to join regardless of this standard.

Gardnerian Witchcraft placed an emphasis on the female aspect as the leader and the male equivalent of her choice. In this case, the High Priestess would choose her own High Priest to lead the coven just as the Goddess has her male consort, the God. Initiation can only be done through the High Priestess or High Priest. Gardner's coven willingly participated in nude sessions that were held on the Sabbat, for their full moon meetings, and decided to customize these sessions to formalize the now standard eight festivities on the Wiccan Wheel. These seasonal festivities are:

- Midwinter (Yule) - December 20 -23.

- Imbolc - February 2.

- Vernal Equinox (Ostara) - March 19 - 22.

- Beltane - May 1.

- Midsummer (Litha) - June 19 - 23.

- Lammas/Lughnasadh - August 1.

- Autumnal Equinox (Mabon) - September 21 - 24.

- Samhain (All Saint's Day) - November 1.

This calendar of celebration is mapped around two solstice events and two equinox events, with four quarterly celebrations to mark the mid-way point of each. Even though Gardnerian Wicca practiced a controversial method of honing energy, it is easy to say that many covens have decided to take on other methods of worship.

Chapter 2: Wiccan Rede And Ardanes

The Wicca Rede.

In relation to the founder of Wicca, which was founded back in 1950's England, there were others who took note of Gardner's teachings and combined it with the knowledge they researched on, or already knew and shared those lessons with their fellow coven members worldwide. Among those lessons were eight words that posed as the Wiccan byline on ethics:

"An' it harm none, do what ye will."

These eight words are famously known as the Wiccan Rede, a guideline for fellow Wiccans to live on as they would so long as it doesn't hurt anyone else. However, this wouldn't be heard till 1964 when, while attending a witch's convention, Doreen Valiente spoke these Anglo-Saxon words during a speech about respecting other covens and people in general. These eight words would make their rounds, being repeatedly used in other publications and, at times, without crediting Doreen. As a response to Valiente's Rede, a Connecticut witch named Lady Gwen Thompson (real name Phyllis Thompson) published a piece in an Ostara 1975 (vol. 3, no. 26) volume of Green Egg Magazine named "Wiccan-Pagan Potpourri," where a 26-lined poem called "Rede of the Wiccae," made its debut.

"Being known as the counsel of the Wise Ones:
1. *Bide the Wiccan Laws ye must In Perfect Love and Perfect Trust.*
2. *Live an' let live - Fairly take an' fairly give.*
3. *Cast the Circle thrice about To keep all evil spirits out.*
4. *To bind the spell every time - Let the spell be spake in rhyme.*
5. *Soft of eye an' light of touch - Speak little, listen much.*
6. *Deosil go by the waxing Moon - Sing and dance the Wiccan rune.*

7. *Widdershins go when the Moon doth wane, An' the Werewolf howls by the dread Wolfsbane.*
8. *When the Lady's Moon is new, Kiss thy hand to Her times two.*
9. *When the Moon rides at Her peak Then your heart's desire seek.*
10. *Heed the Northwind's mighty gale - Lock the door and drop the sail.*
11. *When the wind comes from the South, Love will kiss thee on the mouth.*
12. *When the wind blows from the East, Expect the new and set the feast.*
13. *When the West wind blows o'er thee, Departed spirits restless be.*
14. *Nine woods in the Cauldron go - Burn them quick an' burn them slow.*
15. *Elder be ye Lady's tree - Burn it not or cursed ye'll be.*
16. *When the Wheel begins to turn - Let the Beltane fires burn.*
17. *When the Wheel has turned a Yule, Light the Log an' let Pan rule.*
18. *Heed ye flower bush an' tree - By the Lady Blessèd Be.*
19. *Where the rippling waters go Cast a stone an' truth ye'll know.*

20. When ye have need, Hearken not to others greed.
21. With the fool, no season spend Or be counted as his friend.
22. Merry meet an' merry part - Bright the cheeks an' warm the heart.
23. Mind the Threefold Law ye should - Three times bad an' three times good.
24. When misfortune is now, Wear the Blue Star on thy brow.
25. True in love ever be Unless thy lover's false to thee.
26. Eight words ye Wiccan Rede fulfill - An' it harms none, Do what ye will."

Lady Gwen Thompson (1928 - 1986) was a witch from New Haven, Connecticut. She was initiated into the craft by her grandmother, Adriana Porter. When she became an adult, she founded her own coven, the New England Coven of Traditionalist Witches, where she was able to pass on her family's Celtic traditions towards joining members. It was her grandmother whom Lady Gwen not only dedicated but asserted as a hereditary witch with origins in Somerset, England, that this rede was one that was passed down in her family. Lady Gwen also added a blend of modern ideals into it. Lady Gwen's rede is also an easily recognizable creed of the Wiccan faith. Three years later, in 1978, Doreen Valiente published her book *Witchcraft For Tomorrow* in which she addressed the idea of the rede being placed into rhyme.

"This idea has been put into a rhymed couplet called the Wiccan Rede:

>*Eight Words the Wiccan Rede fulfil*
>*An it harms none, do what ye will.*

This can be expressed in more modern English as follows:

>*Eight words the Witches' Creed fulfil:*
>*If it harms none, do what you will."*

Valiente also included a longer version of this new revision in her book and called it *The Witches' Creed*:

"The Witches' Creed

Hear now the words of the witches,
The secrets we hid in the night,
When dark was our destiny's pathway,
That now we bring forth into light.

Mysterious water and fire,
The earth and the wide-ranging air,
By hidden quintessence, we know them,
And will and keep silent and dare.

The birth and rebirth of all nature,
The passing of winter and spring,
We share with the life universal,
Rejoice in the magical ring.

Four times in the year the Great Sabbat
Returns, and witches are seen
At Lammas, and Candlemas dancing,
On May Eve and old Hallowe'en.

When day-time and night-time are equal,
When the sun is at greatest and least,
The four Lesser Sabbats are summoned,
Again witches gather in feast.

Thirteen silver moons in a year are,
Thirteen is the coven's array.

Thirteen times as Esbat make merry,
For each golden year and a day.

The power was passed down the ages,
Each time between woman and man,
Each century unto the other,
Ere time and the ages began.

When drawn is the magical circle,
By sword or athame or power,
Its compass between the two worlds lie,
In Land of the Shades for that hour.

This world has no right then to know it,
And world beyond will tell naught,
The oldest of Gods are invoked there,
The Great Work of magic is wrought.

For two are the mystical pillars,
That stand to at the gate of the shrine,
And two are the powers of nature,
The forms and the forces divine.

The dark and the light in succession,
The opposites each unto each,
Shown forth as a God and a Goddess,
Of this did our ancestors teach.

By night he's the wild wind's rider,
The Horn'd One, the Lord of the shades,
By day he's the King of the Woodlands,
The dweller in green forest glades.

She is youthful or old as she pleases,
She sails the torn clouds in her barque,
The bright silver lady of midnight,
The crone who weaves spells in the dark.

The master and mistress of magic,
They dwell in the deeps of the mind,
Immortal and ever-renewing,
With the power to free or to bind.

So drink the good wine to the Old Gods,
And dance and make love in their praise,
Til Elphame's fair land shall receive us,
In peace at the end of our days.

An Do What You Will be the challenge,
So be it in Love that harms none,
For this is the only commandment,
By Magick of old, be it done."

Unlike Lady Gwen's rede, Valiente's creed was formulated to be recited as part of the Sabbat Rite. This was read when all formed a circle.

This poem was read, followed then by the hallowed eight words of the Wiccan's Rede *"An' it harm none, do what ye will."*

In addition to the Wiccan's Rede, The Rede of the Wiccae, and The Witches' Creed, we have The Law of Three, or otherwise called The Law of Return. This is another ethical facet structured for witches to consider the ramifications of their actions before spell casting as an act of goodness or spite; for what you put out there will return to you three-fold. This is considered the second ethical rule in Wicca or spellcasting in general. The interesting thing about this rule is that it's not exclusively bound to just spellcasting, but the energy in general. In common terms, this is normally referred to as Karma, the cosmic influence responsible for divine consequence. Karma can be seen as one of the great equalizers in terms of maintaining the balance of energy in the universe. Think of it as the Light and Dark side of the Yin and Yang. There will always be an equal balance of both light and dark, yet the point of the three-fold rule is to provide the person spending that energy and intention with a pensive moment to reflect.

The Wiccan Laws (Ardane).
Wiccan Laws (or Craft Laws) were created by Gardner in 1957. These laws were also known as *Gardnerian Ardanes* and were to have been based on the ancient ways, however, it was found they were based on a number of modern things including Gardner's own Book of Shadows. The laws were a mix of modern (for the time) and archaic phrases that dealt with Wicca's theology, advice, and coven security.

Here are the *old* Gardnerian Ardanes (circa 1957) according to *www.oldways.org/ardanes.html*:

1. These laws were made created from the old ways. These laws were made for the Wicca to aid them in their troubles.

2. All Wicca must worship and give thanks to the Goddess and God. Wicca must obey their will since it was said for the good of their being. As forth, a Wicca's place is to give thanks for the Goddess and God.

3. The Goddess and God love we Wicca, just like a man love a woman by loving her. The Wiccan will always show love for the Goddess and God by loving them. Make certain that the temple we form for the Goddess and God, when the Circle is formed, is formed and purified, so that it can be a wonderful home for the Goddess and God to enter.

4. All Wicca must prepare for their worship by purifying themselves in order to be in the presence of the Goddess and God. Always come with love and praise in your heart as you raise the power in your body and send it to the Goddess and God. This is what we have always been taught to us.

5. This is the only way we humans can communicate with the Goddess and God since the Goddess and God cannot assist us humans without the aide of we humans first.

6. The High Priestess and High Priest of their respective covens shall be the representatives for the Goddess and the God as the Goddess and God's support. The High Priestess is the one who will choose the High Priest as she is of the highest rank.

7. It is said that the God himself, kissed her feet five times in praise and prostrated his power at the feet of the Goddess for it was her youthful beauty, her sweet kindness, her sense of justice and words of wisdom, her giving humble nature that the God prostrated and gave his power to her. The Priestess should always stay humble in light of God's power given to her. God only gives it when wisdom and justice are present. The High Priestess' greatest asset is her youth as it represents the youth of the Goddess and so she may retire when older to make room for a newer and younger High Priestess should her coven vote on it. A true High Priestess will take this on gracefully as an embodiment of one of the virtues and sacrifice her pride in exchange for another in order to find her place again at another time.

8. In the ancient world, when we Witches were accepted, we were accepted and able to worship in some of the greatest temples. Nowadays we must accept our plight and hold our glorious worship in secret.

9. Let it the Ardane be that no one but a Wicca may know of the coven secrets for the enemy is of the many and we may expose ourselves when placed into danger. Let it be Ardane that all covens will not know where another coven is or who their members are, all except the High Priestess and her High Priest. Only when it is safe and secure can the covens meet since, in celebration, we shall have great festivities. We shall not ask where the others came from or give real names.

10. If the time comes when you are in danger; even in the face of extreme pain, you will not expose us.

11. Let the Ardane be that none will speak of the spellwork that came from a Wicca, nor will you give any names or where they live or give any information that can lead to betrayal and an attack from our enemies. If anyone breaks these rules, even under the pain of torture, may the Goddess fully curse them so that they are never to be reborn on earth.

12. Each High Priestess is the leader of her coven. She governs as she maintains a sense of love and justice for she is the one who also consults with the elders and heading advice the Messenger of the Goddess and God when it comes.

13. The High Priestess will listen to all complaints of coven members and try to settle the problems between them. It must be known that even as coven members, we may not agree or see eye-to-eye. Disputes happen.

14. Just because you disagree doesn't make the other person a bad, they may have good ideas, and those ideas should be brought before the coven. If the member does not agree with the coven, or if they refuse to worship under the leadership of the High Priestess, it has to be said, by our laws, and for the sake of convenience for the coven members in the face of avoiding such conflict, that any deflecting member is free to find a new coven, especially if they live farther away from the coven or they are about to move away from said coven. Any person wishing to form their own coven within the confines of the Covendom shall discuss this with the Elders. After which they are immediately removed from the coven to a new Covendom. Other members wishing to join newly formed covens, may do so by removing themselves from their old coven entirely. Elders from both covens shall meet to peacefully discuss coven boundaries.

15.   Other spellcasters who are not part of a coven or the Covendom may join either as they are, but they are not allowed to join both. With the consent of the Elders, we may meet for festivities in the true name of peace and brotherly love. To split a coven means to bring strife. It is for this reason that these laws were created long ago. May the Goddess fully curse those who dishonor them, so let it be Ardaned.

16.   Make sure to keep your book of shadows to yourself. Write within this book of your own makings and allow others to share if they so choose. Always keep this book beside you and never keep someone's book for your own as their own writings are theirs to understand, interpret, and learn from.

17.   Guard your book well and destroy it if you are threatened or attacked. Always do your best to know your book by heart so you can remember what is written, because when the danger is gone, you can create a new book using your saved knowledge. It is for this reason that if any should pass on, destroy their book if it has not already. If one were to find it, it would be used as a weapon against them. So always get rid of unnecessary things. If you are found with your book, it will be used against you as proof of your craft. You may be tortured, so keep all thoughts of the inner working of the craft from your mind.

18.   If torture is too much for you to handle, only say "I will confess. I cannot take this any longer. Tell me what you want me to say and I will say it." If they want you to speak of the coven, do not. If they accuse you of falsities like flying on broomstick, sex with their Christian devil, child sacrifice, or cannibalism; in order to have relief from torture say: "I had a horrible dream and I was not myself. I was confused and couldn't control my actions."

19.   Not all law officials are bad. There are those who only need a reason to show you mercy. If you already confessed, deny it. Say you were under the pain of torture and had to speak; that you were just saying anything to get them to stop. Even if they condemn you, do not fear. The Covendoms hold a strong bond and they may help you escape, just remain resilient till then.

20.   If you already betrayed us, then you're already damned, in this life or the next; you will face an eternal life burning, rotting from the inside, and feeling without. You will won't be able to die peacefully and be embraced by the ecstasy of the Goddess.

21.   It's likely that before you are tortured, you will be drugged. Always understand that Christians fear so much that many die under torture. Fainting is the first sign they've caused, and so they will stop. The tormentors will be likely to feign any torture onto you, but they won't. So do your best to not die.

22.   If you are given drugs, that means there is an ally around that can help you escape. So do not despair. If the worst comes and you are set to burn, wait until the smoke is high enough and bend your head over and inhale deeply. Try to choke and die quickly so you may wake up in the embrace of the Goddess.

23.   To avoid getting found out, let your witch tool be regular ordinary items that other people have in their homes. Make Pentacles out of wax so you may break them easily. Never have a sword unless you have a status that gives you one. Never have any names or signs on things you use for the craft.

24.   To consecrate your vessels and signs with their intended, write their names on them, bless them, and wash it off immediately after. Never engrave as they can be discovered. Let your hints stay visible only to yourself so you may know which is which. Remember, we are the Hidden Children of the Goddess and God, so never do them dishonor.

25. Never brag, never be aggressive, never wish ill will unto others. If anyone in or outside of the coven try to talk to you about the craft, tell them: "Don't talk to me about that stuff. It scares me. I find it to be evil." This is to stave off Christian spies. They speak as though they have experience and as if they have attended the meetings. They would say things like: "My mother was part of a coven. They would worship the Old Ones. I wished I could go myself." For this, always deny all knowledge.

26. To others, it's silly to speak of witches who can fly on broomstick as a witch has to be very light. Others also try to say that all witches are nearsighted old hags, so what is the point of going to these witch meetings? As such, people continue with their remarks. Many of their religious leaders now say that no such people exist, even as a joke. In the future, maybe this persecution against use will fade away and we will be able to worship in peace and security again. So let us all pray for that day to come.

27. May those who honor the blessings of the Goddess and God be the ones who kept with these Ardanes.

28. If the coven has any income, let all members guard it and help it stay clear for the good of the coven since all monies gained is income for the coven. If there are members who earned it, it is their right to be paid what they are owed. Let it be known this is not money used for the craft, but for their own use as hard working individuals. As the Christians say: "Let your work speak for you." If there are any members who willingly work for the coven without pay, then it is a true honor. So let it be Ardane.

29. If there are arguments among the coven members, the High Priestess shall immediately speak to the Elders to speak about the matter. Both parties will be heard, first alone and them together. Neither side is favored, both are judged fairly and just.

30. In the event that there are members who will never agree or others who cannot make fair and just rulings; to those who always seek power for oneself there is but one answer; leave the coven and go elsewhere. Or make your own coven and take those who agree with you along. For those who cannot be a fair and just leader, there is an answer for you; people will leave your unjust ways and you will be alone. No one will want to attend meetings with those they find friction with and can never agree on anything; for your coven to survive, be just. Let it be Ardane.

31. In the ancient days, when witches were of power and reverence, our crafts were used towards those who treated us well. However, in these dark times, we cannot allow ourselves to do this since our enemies have created pits of everlasting fire into which they say their God would cast all people who worship him unless you were among those released by one of their priests' spells and mass. This is mainly done by giving money and lofty gifts to him in order to gain his favor for their great God is always in need of money.

32. As our Goddess and God is in need of our aid to produce fertile humans and crops, so it is the Christian God's need of humans to seek us out and destroy us. Their priests tell them as an edict that those who help us or seek our help with illness will be cast into their Hell for eternity. This drives their men mad with terror, so they make them believe they can escape if they give witches to the tormentors. It is for the very reason they spy on us, hoping that if they can catch just one of us, that they will be spared the fiery pits.

33. We Wicca have our hideouts, and yet men continue to search for us only to find nothing. It's not until one of their own dies or gets ill when they cry and blame us, saying "it's the malice of the witches," and their hunt begins again. And though they have done themselves harm by killing ten of their own to one of ours, still they run amok for while they have thousands, we are only a few.

34. Let it be Ardane that no ill will be done to any from those who practice or use crafts no matter how hurt we may be. So long as we obey this law: "harm no one," in time people may believe we no longer exist. So let it be Ardane that this law shall continue to protect us no matter our plight. "No matter what injury you've acquired. No matter the injustice you've wrought. One should not use your craft to do harm or ill will to others."

35. We may not be able to harm none, as say our edict, but with great consultations with all in the coven, our craft can be used to prevent or restrain Christians from doing harm to us and others, and only that. It is not used to punished as that is cause for harm and ill will. Many people have died due to the harm and blame others have caused onto them. In England, it has been many a year since a witch has died. However, we must still be careful as any misuse of the craft can lead to persecution again. So never break this law. If you know it's being broken, then you must fight against it, strongly. If any High Priestess or High Priest are consenting to this behavior, then they must leave the coven immediately for it is the unity and love of the coven and the member of the coven they are endangering. So make sure to stick to the old laws and never accept money for your craft for that money will corrupt those who accept it. It is the incarcerators, conjurers, and priests of Christ that are hungry for money and will allow you use of their arts. Accepting money for your craft will instill more temptation to use the craft for evil purposes. So let the coven discuss this at great length and detail and if all are fine with it harming none, then let the craft be used. So if you cannot find a way of obtaining your goals one way, then maybe you can obtain them in a different manner so that none are harmed. So let it be Ardane.

36. Let it be known that when finding a house or land, and no one is willing to sell, that it is encouraged to persuade the owner into willfully selling without doing them any harm. Let it be known that you will provide the full pay without the need to bargain down the price. So never cheapen that which you intent to use for craft or live in. So let it be Ardane.

37.   It is laid in the old law, and the most important of those laws, that none may endanger the lives of any one from the coven or expose them to the law of the country, or the law of the church or any of our enemies. No matter the argument within a coven, none shall incite any other law but those of the coven and any rulings given by the High Priestess, the High Priest, and the Elders. And that the full curse of the Goddess is on those who do. So let it be Ardane.

38.   Because of the old ways of Christianity, our oppressors made it an affront to their God to not believe Witchcraft exists, and thus a crime to deny. Therefore it is okay to say as the Christians do: "there are witches among us in this land," and keep yourself out of suspicion. Always speak in order to cast doubt that they are near and that they're old hags who dwell in dark places and commune with the Christian devil and flying in the air. Always ask how men can fly through the air if they're not as light as a small plant? May the full curse of the Goddess be on those who toss suspicion on their fellow coven members, speak of meeting places, or where other members live. Let it be Ardane.

39.   Let the Covendom keep records of all herbs that are good for people, and all cures so that we may learn from them. And let the Elders keep another book with all the poisonous plants and herbs so that those we trust can guard this knowledge. Let it be Ardane.

40.   Let the blessings of the Goddess and God be upon those who keep these laws intact. May the curses of both the Goddess and the God be fully met on those who dishonor them. Let it be Ardane.

Since then, many versions of these laws have come into being due to outdated terms and non-politically correct laws. A newly revised version of craft laws was created by Lady Galadriel. These ardanes were taken and reworded from four books of craft law she researched: *The Book of the Law, The Old Laws for the Old Religion, The Great Book of the Law, and The Dragon Law.* She used her knowledge of teaching groups, leading groups, and these books to create a new standard for today's world in her own book of law called *The New Book of the Law.*

The New Book of the Law.

1.   Laws were given to man to help them give purpose and meaning to their lives. It provides the balance for us on all realms of existence. The truth is, we have two sets of laws: one that educates us on Wiccan ways, the other is the universe itself. Wiccans cannot exist without form and order, and we cannot exist without the blessings of the universe for these are aspects that provide us counsel, advice, and education in our lives on this planet.

2.   Always give thanks and praise to the Goddess and God for that shows honor. Honor them and be blessed with the source of your energy that lies within you. Love the Goddess and God by loving yourself and your coven. You will be loved in return as it blooms as it grows taller. Shower it with respect and take in the understanding and honor you have shown for the Goddess and God.

3.   Our Goddess is our Great Mother as is the God, our Great Father. We Wicca are their children, and as children, we shall worship them for they are our universe and we are within it. So, children of our Goddess and God, do not test them as they will punish you for mocking your lessons. Be aware children, the ways of the craft are never to be mocked or dismissed.

4.   Embrace the power of the craft from within you and let it flow with love and nothing else. The energy we create spins around in many ways, creating webs woven to eventually encircle us as it always goes back to its origin. You. Therefore we are either entangled and bound by our actions, or we're embraced by which the Goddess and God have blessed us with.

5.   Let our power flow as children of the Goddess and God as we relish under the light of the Rites of Wicca and come together as one. We should always honor and respect the Earth. We shall heal her when sick or injured. We shall tend to her needs by providing power and undying love to her. She is our Goddess, she is our Great Mother. She is the ship we ride upon and plot our course to help guide us through rough and torrential tides of space and time.

6.   The fruits of your labor are harvested, not from one portion but the entire field. Do not shorten yourself to one corner or section of your garden. These are your blessings, taken them all and offer great thanks to our Earth Mother either directly onto your altar, the Circle, or by way of the High Priestess and High Priest.

7. Be proud of who you are as a Wicca, but never flourish with vanity. Those who display conceit block their own path towards the temple and will never truly make it in. They will be swept away in it and eventually forget their love.

8. Patiently listen. Quietly observe. Let judgement stay still until all things have been considered and values weighed.

9. Good tidings beget those who do good. You will be rewarded if you genuinely bring love and joy with you. As like breeds like, so does a good hug.

10. The High Priestess and High Priest, are the servants of the Goddess and God. It is their duty to seed the soil of your mind with knowledge and to use their power for the good of the coven. Make sure to tend the seeds and fertilize the soil when things have been planted. Let them germinate and sprout for they will turn into a most bountiful harvest. Those who misuse this trust will lose position with their teachers and coven leaders and will have to endure the answer Karma has for them.

11. All Circles are a family. And all families of Wicca are children to the Goddess and God. Their temples are their homes and their homes are the Circles we call family. Never slight the temple nor your Wicca family unless you want the Goddess and God against you.

12. Never lie to we children of the Goddess and God. You must never hold a grudge or dark thoughts against anyone of the Wicca.

13. Elders bring additional wisdom, so never lie to them or falsely accuse another before them. You will be a liar and a fool and a chaotic mess unto yourself and your love as a Wicca. Be true, be truthful in all that you do and say within and out of the Circle for what you put out there will come back in the manifest.

14. Never show malice, spite, or prejudice towards those who do not follow the Wicca way. You must never believe yourself more righteous than others, but you should help them with love when it's needed. If you ever console the Elders and say nothing to others about where we have our meetings, nor should you reveal our ways without their consent or the consent of the High Priestess.

15.   Professing a vow to a Lord or Lady, or swearing a promise to another Wicca, then one must do all that they've confessed to do as this is seen as a covenant with between the Goddess, the God, and the Circle. Your honor is your word. Your actions should speak in the stead of your words. Your soul is attached to your words.

16.   The Ancient and Mighty Ones shall cause the balance to be made for those who desecrate the Lord and Lady, Their temples, or Their creations. Our Great Mother and our Great Father are ancient and almighty. We as their children are precious to them and would never want to see us suffer in their names. As you see, what lies in the heart and souls of the children is true for the parent.

17.   Wicca will never cause harm. Never use magic for harm as this is an abuse of the power gifted to you and is never supported. To hurt and be the cause of a death through the craft is to place yourself as a sacrificial death.

18.   The lore of our people and your coven family are all sacred and should never be betrayed. We are all servants of the Goddess and God and must abide by the virtues of honoring the love and wisdom bestowed upon us. *Let the creed of loyalty and truth walk with honor and guide you.*

19.   Believe when you truly believe. Keep the Order of the Gods intact and say "I believe," when you walk into their Circles. Never profess what sounds right when you don't believe from the inside. Believe first, then walk into the Temple.

20.   The Goddess and God love all their children, so never dishonor their love by using dark emotions to speak their names to hurt others as the Goddess and God love even those who are unaware of them, yet those who use their names to curse shall have their worth lessened by the Almighty Ones.

21.   Any disagreements between the coven members shall be assessed within the coven or by the High Priestess or High Priest, or the Elders.

22.   No Wicca shall engage in things that will endanger the Arts, the Craft, or the coven. Nor will you engage the Wicca way into the law of the country or our persecutors for fear of conflict.

23.   Magical tools are your channels in strengthening your connection with the Goddess and God. Never cheapen their importance by pawning them off.

24.   Do not sell your power for the highest bidder. It is those posing as sorcerers, the charlatans, who willingly accept money for their power. Accepting no money means freedom from the dark temptation of using your gift to hurt others or shallow causes.

25.   Never steal things that you do not own. An order to balance will be needed if you do. If you take that which does not belong to you, then you will have something more precious taken from you for balance to be realized again.

26.   The opinions of you are shown in the eyes of others. So respect and show them honor lest you not be shown respect and honor in return.

27.   Wicca shall never enslave others for the spirit of another is own by our Great Mother and our Great Father. One should never pledge to take another person's life for this is a great betrayal and you will forever curse yourself.

28.   If an outsider stays with you, never do them any harm and yet treat them as you would your Circle. They are equal to you like you were born side by side. Treat them as you would treat yourself.

29.   The Laws of Three will be recognized as the Universe is always just and will always maintain due balance.

30.   Tend to your altars with love and care. Keep them pure and sacred for this signifies your love to keep the home of the Goddess and God as well as your Circle a sacred and holy place to worship.

31.   Honor our Great Mother and keep yourself, your garments, and your dwellings clean.

32.   Pay respects to those who have passed on with love, honor, and respect unless decreed by the leaders of the coven.

33.   Do not engage in coupling for the sole intention of harming another or greed. Such unions are considered malice and it is this dark reasoning that will cause the Universe to seek an adjustment for balance as well as harm the coven.

34.   Let those who love, love true and be as one. Be joined in matrimony and bear children for the joining of two souls into one is the most beautiful energy we can honor the Goddess and God with. Let our children know about the aspects that gave them life.

35. The laws of our Great Mother, the Goddess, is to wish that no Wicca shall choose someone to wed if they do not love them for this will do harm to you and the other, especially if this is for material gain.

36. We are children of the Goddess and the God and as such, your children also come from their loins and are free, not controlled. Treat your children with love and they may come and visit for one day they may also pass on this love and wisdom you have shown them. Guide them, care for them, and aid them.

37. The needs of Earth are always in motion, creating vortices and webs of energy to help it adjust to its needs. The duty of we Wicca are sacred in that it is within us to channel the Universal force to create agencies of light and schools of knowledge with the divine magic given to us. It is the realms of both the stars and earth that creates a relationship that brings in and maintains the flames of the spirits who activate the life of this world. So we need to guard and nurture those very threads and weave a way of life to thread itself onto a tapestry that continues to flourish.

38. Heritage for the sake of position or glorification is looked down upon. Respect is in how you treat your craft and the Wicca way. One must always see that while we all need others to help guide us, that those guides will also need guidance themselves.

39. Keep your goals as pure and chaste as your body, mind, and belief for this is used to channel your power. This power must be as strong and pure as your conviction. That is the key to knowing oneself and communing with the Goddess and God. Speak to them as you will be able to understand what they say as they will understand you. We of the Wicca, the children of our Great Mother and our Great Father, we must assist them, or the Goddess and the God cannot work with us. Always remember, that the High Priestess and High Priest are the closest representatives to our Goddess and God. Remember the life force the represent as we humans also have these forces within ourselves, waiting to be awakened.

40. Create a place to welcome our Great Mother and our Great Father by representing their energies within your sacred spaces. Invite the Goddess and God with the energy for love and wisdom. Our Circle should be purified before being cast, just like any entries for travel using the Circle to come and go between the earth realm and others should also prepare themselves with purification and preparedness before traversing.

41.   And our Great Mother as said, "I cannot shelter you, nor shall I keep you from exploring, nor will I hurt your opportunities as you have the same as do all my children. Be free yet seek me out when in need. If you have the truest devotion within oneself, then your obstacles will be easily won."

42.   If half the work is what you seek, then half of the reward is what one wins. While something is better than nothing at all, doing the whole thing lands you the entire pot. Those who lack this conviction to learn of our Goddess and God is said, "Of the Almighty and of the Olden Ones will not keep thou for long if ye are not astute towards learning."

43.   Make your dwelling into a dwelling fit for the Goddess and God to enter. Regard it to the best of your knowledge, love, energy, and according to the Elder teachings.

44.   Come unto the Goddess, the Lady, by making an altar to show her reverence. The exalted Goddess, our Great Mother, will come and bless you. An altar from wood or stone and tools where burning incense and candles during her proper times will be looked upon and loved.

45. Love the Goddess every day, yet properly address her at least once a month. It is on those days that you shall listen and assist her, and it is on that day where the Goddess will renew you, her child, and bless you.

46. Learn the ways to create and build your own Temple and to cast your own Circle and understand all the tools needed, for this is how one of the craft understands consequence.

47. Write your own record of your learning and thoughts. The way of the Wicca should be recorded so that the paths in their life may be seen and known for others to take heed from. Each Wiccan can start their own Book of Light and fill it with teaching and olden lore of their individual tradition, but let it also holds the ways and rites that were harvested for the sake of tradition and let this be used to pass on the wisdom and heritage to enrich the lives of others and themselves if they so wish.

48. Pursue your studies to understand sigils, the lore of the Goddess and God, and effigies of their visage as they will help you guide your thoughts to them. Your communication will be clearly heard by them so long as you continue to worship the Goddess and God that inspire those tales, statues, and signs.

49. Let all that love the Circle, protect it. If the Circle is on land you own, let all within guard it and tend to it. Let all members justly protect the monies of the Circle as well as justly providing protection to property members may own.

50. If any Wiccan is under employment, then it is their just due to being paid what they earned. The money is not taken for the craft, but for services rendered. However, if any Wicca does so voluntarily for the good of the coven, then this is a great honor onto them.

51. A Wiccan who remains physically chaste and spiritually humble in the service of the Circle, then said a person will be blessed and always remembered. To those who give for the good of the Circle are those who will have their spirits lifted.

52. Let it be known that if you present gifts for the Goddess's High Priestess and High Priest, or the Circle, then the gift is an offering made towards our Great Mother for a High Priestess and High Priest will always do her work and represent her to help nurture her children. Therefore it is of their true directive to honor and respect the will of the Goddess.

53. And the Goddess and God are pleased with simple offerings like fruit fresh from an orchard, the scent of trees and ripe herbs, the metals and waters the earth, flowers swaying in their meadows, and the nurturing milk that comes from mothers. While offerings hard work or money are welcomed, it is more if you have worked with love as there is always work to be had in the service of the Goddess and God as well as your work within the Circle.

54. If offerings are made with the intention to restore a balance, then is needs to be in the nature that is not offensive to our Great Mother and our Great Father. The value must be given of your heart; thus the harmony will be restored. Your heart carries the weight of which you give as an offering since it is this message that will be carried to the Goddess and God. And that message should be of love and devotion to the coven and first to the Goddess and God. Be blessed for your blessings will come.

55. Offerings are to be made to the Goddess and God at the proper time and in a proper manner in order to be accepted. When one is finished with the ritual, all remnants shall be burned or buried in the soil to symbolize all things returning to the source of observance from us to the Goddess and God, and thus providing our continued connection.

56. The Circle is there to protect and aid the coven members so long as the advantage you seek does no harm to no one else. Each Wicca and Circle will convene for discussion to help sort these matters at length. If all are satisfied that no one will be harmed, then the craft can be used. If this cannot be done to achieve a member's goal, then maybe the goal is one that takes a different method of achieving so that none will be harmed.

57. In today's world, it has been years and years since Wiccans were placed into fiery pits, however, arrogance can lead to a misuse of our power which might bring about persecutions again. Therefore it needs repeating to never forgo the laws no matter how tempted or hurt you might be. Work strongly against it if you know a law is being broken to protect us.

58. In days of yore, it was decided by the coven, High Priestess and High Priest, and Elders, that using the craft to protect the Wicca from persecution was allowed. This was only done after great consultation and considerations from the need to deflect attention or constrain them without doing harm.

59. Let all be of joy and let all be of beauty as you offer love in your worship to the Goddess as she, our Great Mother, has enveloped us in her joy. Let us offer love in our life and all of its pleasure as we offer this love to the God, our Great Father, for he blessed us to understand the pleasure that is life itself.

60. In ancient times, we Wiccan were free of persecution. Atlantis came and an age of the misuse of power came to be. This followed an age of religious persecution and torture. And thus the children of the Goddess and God had to hide themselves, and in doing so cloaked any knowledge they previously shared with the world and spoke in secret verse while in public but cloaked in shadow when set to meet. This was the only way the Wicca of old could persevere through the dark times even though much of our ways were lost to ignorance and fear brought on by others.

61. As the cycle continues, the dawn of the Earth Mother draws closer. To be within our birthright, and to be with our Great Mother and our Great Father, we must remain strong so the balance will be realized. People who seek to harm us in an effort to enslave or destroy who we are is something we must overcome through light and love. Never, regardless of the trials, overcome using violence and dark chaos. In those efforts, our time will come into fruition once more. We have much work to be done in the time that remains ahead. When the time is right, the cycle will begin again when the path of light attracts it and balance is finally achieved through the energy of love.

62. In an effort to bring the paths of Life, Love, and Light, our ways are slowly becoming public knowledge to the other peoples of this Earth. And this is a good thing since it signals that the days of skulking in shadow and secrecy are fading away. However, the sharing of these ways must be guided by those harboring the wisdom and the love to educate. Let the rites of the Wicca and the secrets of our ways be kept sacred. Never let anyone defile the worship or heritage we've held onto for so long for the defiling of those ways is only an honor lost unto oneself and your craft.

63. All honor the High Priestess who governs her coven as she does this with absolute love and humble justice. As she governs, she is aided by the advice of the Elders and a High Priest of her choosing as they all will heed the words of the Goddess and God when spoken through the Messenger.

64. Always observe that while the High Priest is an aspect of force that builds the Circle, the High Priestess is the leader since it is her that the Goddess molded the world and nurtured all things wherein.

65. It is the High Priestess that will listen to the concerns and complaints of all Pagans and Wiccans alike in an attempt to resolve differences that arise. She will do this with a humble sense of justice and reason.

66. All covens of Light shall decide how they shall be formed, by either using an Earth-based name or a Magic-based one. Each child of Wicca should understand the best ways to stay safe and perceived dangers of their village, town, or city.

67. Let all things needed for rituals done in the Circle or Temple be dedicated to the Goddess and God. May they be blessed in their under the rightful names of the Goddess and God and given to the High Priestess and High Priest to care for them.

68. Those of satisfactory rank who wish to form a coven of their own should speak to the High Priestess and the Elders to tell them of their intentions. If members of the former coven wish to join the new one when if forms, they are free to do so by leaving the one they are currently in unless instructed otherwise. This is the old law that all Wicca may join a coven of their choice yet may not join more than one for their energy cannot be divided into two or more Temples.

69.   Elders of older and newly formed covens shall peacefully meet to establish a new level of interactivity and relations between the two covens. As it is known, a fracture within the coven is a bad omen that brings strife. The only course to mend this fissure is for both covens to meet for a celebratory time of festivities as a sign of union.

70.   None with a corrupted faith or love shall be accepted into the coven for that will be called a sickness and it will cause harm to both the coven and the Goddess and God. It is at this time where the healers should assess the sick and affirm the love of the Goddess and God into them so that they may heal and be well once more.

71.   It has been deemed of law that any of the coven, if in need of a house or land and no one wants to sell, to persuade someone's willingness to sell, on the basis that this will do no harm and the full amount of the asking price is paid without bargaining.

72.   The High Priestess shall convene and inquire in council towards the disputes and arguments between coven members. The council will privately hear both sides separately and then together. The decision will be reached in a just manner, with neither side being favored over the other.

73.   If arguments persist or one refuses the resolution, then the Wicca must leave the coven immediately as a coven cannot function if the Circle cannot be properly formed and the energy harnessed is corrupted. It is our duty to let them leave of their own accord with love in our hearts and for one day our paths may merge again as children of the Great Mother and Great Father. May none leave with grudges or ill will or it will rot one's power from the inside and leave you corrupt.

74.   Just in case we have members who are corrupt and either refuse to work or agree with others or, at the same time, those who are to lead a coven not ruling with the virtues of humility and justice, we have an answer for the one who always wants to take charge; "leave the coven and find another. If you are of rank, form your own." To those who cannot be just in their ruling, your answer is clear: "Wicca who cannot stand your behavior will leave your coven." For this, none are allowed to come into a coven if they present friction on their persona. This will displease the Goddess and God as it will set back the unity of the craft.

75.   Innocence is granted to those who have done wrong without understanding the knowledge behind the decision. If one does wrong by carelessness, then they are judged as lacking wisdom and will be given a rightful due based on the context of the error. Those who intended to be wrong with extra thought given to it shall be punished three fold as Karma dictates.

76. Each Wicca takes an equal responsibility for their words and actions, so in the eyes of the Elders, they will try to salvage a lesson one could learn from it. This places the Wiccan in a position to restore the balance. So listen to the Elders and the High Priestess and High Priest when addressed.

77. Never turn your back on a stranger who wants to learn the ways of Wicca if they have nothing to give or do not come in full attire. Both of you are servants of the Goddess and God, therefore you are equal in their eyes. It is those that search for the Goddess and God that you shall help during their quest.

78. If a stranger wishes to become a Wicca, let their eyes speak, let their spirit reach you, and let the story of their journey convince you of their way for it is not the number of people you want to be in your coven, but those who genuinely want to be there to fulfill their path.

79. We Wicca are the hidden children of the world. We are like harp strings for each of us casts a wonderful note, yet when all are strummed together, we create the most melodic sound. However if we, like strings, are plucked without consideration, our notes may cause harm. It is, therefore, our Great Mother and our Great Father's decree to our coven leaders, Elders, High Priestess, and High Priest, that we all must be taught harmony for in doing so produces thought and care without harm or chaos.

80. Coven leaders like the High Priestess and High Priest, as well as coven teachers, are roles that should be chosen with complete care. If their virtues mirror a mastery of knowledge, faith, patience, humility, leadership, belief, ability, and a pure loving nature, then let it be so for they will lead and teach the children of the Goddess and God and thus have the power to do good or cause a fissure.

81. It is our practice that the High Priestess and the High Priest should guide the rituals set for all Temples for the Goddess and God and therefore bring contentment to you with their sage advice and guidance. However, it should always be known and clear that within all Temples, each Wicca is free and to be able to see and comprehend the ways and implications of each other. If you cannot explain such workings or their decisions, then you may be questioned or the wisdom behind your advice will be reconsidered.

82. The High Priestess and High Priest are to lead as they are allowed, and their ability as leaders will show the wisdom and strength needed to nurture the coven. However, if they are of ill-health, or if it is time for the next generation to take a position, then let them. Pass onto them the vision and wisdom it takes to step away from the position and pass the duties of the coven onto the new generation. Never become too attached to the position or attracted to its power.

83. If a High Priestess or a High Priest would like to step down from their duties, then they may only do so when a successor has been trained and properly acknowledged. If a High Priestess or High Priest deflects from the coven, then they no longer have the right to lead the coven in this life as that trust has been greatly broken. Should they return within the time of the Wheel's turn and have truly atoned by finding a new light and growth from within, then forgiveness is gifted and they are allowed to return to the Circle, but only to worship as a member. No rank or office will be given. To be a leader is a sacred honor that holds a lifetime of commitment that one must take to task respectfully.

84. If a High Priestess, High Priest, or Elder are found to consent in breaking olden laws of no harm from the coven, then they are immediately dismissed of their position as their teachings are the ones that nurture the coven, and as children of the Goddess and God it could lead to corruption and harm endanger us all.

85. If the High Priestess needs time away from her coven for personal reasons, then she is allowed to for up to a year and a day. In which time the Maiden will act in her stead as High Priestess. If said High Priestess cannot or does not return by the end of that time, then coven members shall nominate a new High Priestess. If there is a good reason to, the one who has done the work as the substitute High Priestess shall continue with the position. If another's name comes up, the Maiden will continue as a Maiden.

86. Each High Priestess and High Priest shall choose her or his own consorts for it be wisdom that is sought in the learning of the coven, and therefore the coven shall honor the wisdom of their choice. However, if the coven feels uneasy with the choice, or they believe it is not something they can follow, honor, or form a trust with the chosen consort, then a gathering can be requested of all concerned to discuss and hopefully mend the balance of the coven with love and acceptance. It is only when purity, wisdom, patience, strength, keen, and love are in effect that a coven can properly carry out its teachings and the High Priestess and High Priest can carry out their duties as Keepers of the Coven.

87. *Let those of the Priesthood balance out their lives between nurturing the coven and nurturing their personal life. Be it health, material things, or the needy, none should be neglected for the sake of the coven. Thus adjusting for both families is necessary so that neither is neglected, for that given by the Goddess and God is honored with love and respect.*

88. *At the dawn of time, a very long time ago, it was understood that the female shall have the power of giving life. And thus the male-force was drawn in by the female-force for he loved her beauty when she created life and the love she exuded. Immediately he surrendered to her and focused his force to only further life. The High Priestess must always regard that which fuels the flames that light her senses from within her Temple is to come from her High Priest. Therefore this force is to be used by her wisely as it's only with love that she must honor and respect the one who activates that life force.*

Chapter 3: The Divinity Of Wicca

The Dark History Of Paganism.

The history behind Wicca's definition as the first of its kind in inscribing multiple traditions into a formulaic rite in the modern era has caused quite the controversy among researchers who are interested in unearthing the true origins of those professing to be descended from witches or have a continued practice in their familial line as a witch, but particularly those who claim they have lineage from the infamous Witch-Cult cited by Margaret Murray in her articles. Despite this, paganism is still rife with bad rumors stemming from centuries old events and harbored ill-conceived notions. For instance, the Pentacle, or commonly known as a Pentagram, has been used since the ancient days of Sumeria, Babylon, Greece, China, Japan, and in some religious sects like Judaism and early Christianity. Normally it's just a five-point star denoting one's faith, healthy body, or the elements. There were even instances within some of those cultures where the pentagram was revered as a magical symbol. Here were some of the beliefs the Pentagram held:

- Christianity (without the circles) - represents the five senses, the five wounds of Christ, or could also be symbolic of the Alpha and Omega before being replaced by the cross. This symbol could also be traced back to the Arthurian tale of Sir Gawain and the Green Knight, describing the upstanding virtues of knighthood as being close with Jesus Christ's sacrifice. This is known as the five virtues: generosity, courtesy, chastity, chivalry, and piety.
- Ancient Babylon - a representation of their various gods and religious beliefs. Some of those beliefs include the five senses and the five known planets (at the time): Jupiter, Mercury, Mars,

Saturn, and Venus (also known as Ishtar - Queen of Heaven). The pentagram also represented the forwards, backwards, left, right, and above.

- China and Japan - represents the elements of life. For Japan, it is also a symbol of magic.
- Egypt and Celts - represented the underground womb, from which all life originates.
- Druids - represents the Godhead.
- Greece - was used by Pythagoras, however, it also represented the Greek goddess of health, Hygieia. When used inverted, it represented the five chambers of Pentemychos, a place in Tartaros where pre-cosmic offspring had to be placed in order for the ordered cosmos to appear.

The last use of the inverted Pentagram (Greece) could very well have been a tool in what 19th century author, Eliphas Levi, called it evil.

Levi was an influential writer of the 19th century, and due to his views many social stigmas on ancient symbolism had their original meaning either rewritten or reinvented to suit particular views. His most iconic view of the purpose of the inverted pentagram as the sigil of Baphomet. In 1855, Levi associated the imagined deity with a Sabbatic Goat. He even described the inverted pentagram in *Transcendental Magic, It's Doctrine And Ritual* in such a way that describes it as goat-like: "*A reversed pentagram, with two points projecting upwards, is a symbol of evil and attracts sinister forces because it overturns the proper order of things and demonstrates the triumph of matter over spirit. It is the goat of lust attacking the heavens with its horns, a sign execrated by initiates.*"

In short, Wiccans have nothing to do with worshiping the devil. So take it as you will, you don't have to feel guilty if you decide to wear a pentagram. It has many definitions from representing the five human senses to a representation of the Gods of Babylon. In Wicca, a pentagram represents protection for one-self and is worn the same way a Christian wears a crucifix.

The Goddess And The God.
The Wiccan Divinity involves the Goddess and her male consort the Horned God. The Triple Goddess is an aspect of the Goddess; the Maiden, the Mother (often seen as pregnant, and the Crone. Both Goddess and Horned God also have astrological aspects where the Goddess represents the Moon, and the Horned God represents the Sun; polarities of the other. This is why you see the Triple Goddess represented as moon phases and the Horned God as The Sun God.

In addition to the Wiccan Goddess and God, are there iterations descended from other ancient cultures. For instance, while the Goddess can represent any Goddess that fulfills your goals and needs, you can still justify her as a goddess of the moon and look for other "moon goddesses" to find their names. One that stands out is the Roman goddess, Diana; Greek goddess, Artemis; Native American goddess, Athenesic; South American goddess, Auchimalgen; Babylonian goddess, Anunit; Celtic goddess, Arianrhod (inspired the Wheel of the Year as her name means silver-wheel); and lastly the Kenyan and Ugandan goddess, Arawa. All lunar goddesses hold different roles within their individual cultures, however, it's good to note that a little investigation will lead you to see the link between some of these moon goddesses, and the one represented in the Wiccan faith. The same can be said of the Horned God.

The Horned God also has many iterations as the Sun God. In Greece, the Horned God is the deity known as Pan. In the Celtic faith, the Horned deity is known as Cernunnos. In Rome, he is Faunus, and in India, he is known as Pashupati. The Sun God portion of this god also has many names. In Egypt, her is known as Amun. In Greece, Helios; Inti, from the Incan Empire; Tonatiuh, from the Aztecs; and Malakbel, from Arabic mythology.

Just like the Goddess is a representation of all Goddesses, the Horned God has other faces within the Wiccan faith. The Green Man of the Forest, and the Holly & Oak Kings. While the Green Man represents the seasonal cycle and reverence for nature, the Holly and Oak kings are the twin aspects. While one rules, the other rests. While one is strong, the other is weak. Each rule for a half a year. The Holly King is often portrayed as a somewhat forest version of Santa Claus; sprigs of Holly dangling in and out of his hair dresses in red and is sometimes seen driving eight stags. Whereas the Oak King is also seen as the Green Man. He is portrayed as a God of fertility and is the lord of the forest. One could say that these three aspects represent the youth to an elder aspect of life as well. However, my favorite depiction of the Horned God is one of simplicity. It's of a hunter with antlers emerging from his head.

Chapter 4: Your Start With Wicca

As your curiosity for Wicca grows stronger, it's okay to look up Wiccan covens online. No matter how much you gather from this or any other books on Wiccan ways, you should always be aware that true learning comes from experience and tutelage than a written account of someone's work. Your strength as a Wiccan should be seen with experienced eyes that can help you grow. Even if you're not fond of groups and choose to work as a solitary, it's still a good idea to have a coven leader as a teacher. However, if you so choose, you may only want to nurture your gift on your own. If that is the case, then may you be blessed on your journey for knowledge. There are a lot of books to research and a lot of practice you would have to do in order to get to where you want to be. So for starters, let's start with the very basics you would need to know.

- Setting up your altar.

- Honing your energy.

- Your Wiccan tools.

In this chapter, I will only focus on methods to help you hone your energy through visualization, raising, and grounding techniques, as well as basics in meditation. Spellcasting will not be part of this chapter.

Your altar.
When getting your altar ready, there are some things to consider. Do you want this altar indoors or outdoors? Which direction should my altar face? Where should I place my altar? What items should I have for the Goddess side, the God side, the middle, and do I want to add anything extra?

Your altar should be in a place where you feel relaxed. This is going to be useful in times when you want to meditate, visualize, pray, bless items, spells, or if you just want to talk to the goddess and god. Placing this inside or outside depends on two things, how comfortable you are and if you're able to. If you can't have your altar outside because you live in an apartment building or you feel there is no sacred space for you to call your own, then it's okay to set one up inside your house. Next is choose where. Normally a bedroom is a perfect place since its private and it's the one place where we can normally relax. So choose which direction you want your altar to face. This can be based on a number of things. You can have the altar facing a direction directly connected to your astrological element. You can have it facing North to North-East in connection towards the usual direction practitioners begin their rituals. You can have it facing the numerical equivalent to the time of your birth. You can even have it facing the seasonal direction of the season you were born in. It's completely up to you how you want this altar to represent your needs. After you have decided, next is to find something to place it on. This is entirely up to you. If you feel you want the altar to be represented on a surface you feel empowers you, then go for it. Remember this altar is the connection between your faith and the deities.

Next is knowing what to place on the altar. First, you must represent the Goddess and the God; then the middle and any extras you feel are relevant to your goals and connection. Remember to choose the style of the altar you are making. This means if you feel you have a cultural connection to a particular goddess in Egyptian, Native American, Celtic, or another cultures' lore, then use their symbolism to set up your altar to respect them.

The Goddess side normally uses an effigy of the Goddess you feel connected to, a large candle in the color you feel represents your Goddess, something that represents the feminine aspect of the Goddess (look up the symbolism for your goddess), Crystal balls or other divination tools (tarot cards, runes, scrying mirror, pendulum, dream book…etc.), objects that you personally find sacred or special.

The God side is set up using the same premise. So please look up and choose the appropriate symbolism for the God you feel connected to. A difference between this and the Goddess is that you would have to choose an appropriate object for two masculine elements.

The middle of your altar is the area you'll most use, so place your patron deity and their objects there. Your go-to items there as well (like divination tools, spell casting tools, incense, candles…etc.). You can also have other aspects of your worship like your Book of Shadows, candles, wands (God aspect), Athame (God aspect), Pentacle (Goddess aspect), stones or crystals, or talismans. Whatever objects you decide to use, make sure they have a strong connection to you and your patron deity. Extra items can also be placed on the altar as well.

Honing Your Energy.

So now that you have your altar set up, let's start with getting your energy flowing. Two ways to do this are to visualize your energy flowing throughout your body and to incorporate an activity or an area where you feel your energy is bringing you the most confidence and assertion throughout your body and attitude. Raising your energy is important for spellcasting, rituals, ceremonies, prayers, circles, and divination. However, it's just as important to let all that energy flow away after you're finished. This is where grounding is used. Too much active energy still remains after doing a spiritual work. This can lead to discomfort as your body will experience tensions, aches, or odd sensations in some areas. If this active energy continues to remain, it could lead to illness and lethargy. Yes, it does have the ability to sap energy. So remember, as you summon the energy, so much you let it go into the earth. So your thanks for the deities who provided you with the boost and thanks to the earth for taking it out and away from your body.

Visualization is exactly what it sounds like. One is placed into a relaxed state, closes their eyes, taking deep yet calming breaths. You let your consciousness drift throughout your body, letting it understand your body's layout as you start to slightly feel tingling sensations. At this time you should practice feeling the energy in your body. Practice feeling the energy in your toes. What you want to accomplish is feeling your energy working its way up your body to the crown of your head. Visualizing your energy any way that works for you and getting a good feel for the energy in your body will take practice. This helps you understand how it's flow works in your body.

So after you've finished your casting or prayer, there's active energy left over. What you want to do is now ground the energy. This means you're directing the energy you've worked up to go into the ground where it will be absorbed into the earth. This works by visualizing and feeling. Again, in a relaxed state, direct your energy to go downward towards your feet. Now you're going to feel it's presence leave your feet and into the ground below. You will start to feel a connected sensation. This is called rooting. This is the connection of your human form extending into the ground. Tell the energy to go into the earth. Wish it a farewell and what you wish it to do to help the earth. You should start feeling calmer. When this happens, you can stop. Say your blessings and thanks.

In addition to your altar and your energy practice, there are your craft tools. These are your instruments, or your tool kit, for the moments you cast or bless, or protect. Every worker has them. It could be one or many things. This is up to you based on what you're spiritually attracted to. Tools like wands, feather wands, specialized bowls, fans, talismans, dream catchers, mortar and pestle, incense, chimes, books of scripture, white cloth can be used. There are also disposable ingredients to help aid in such things like oils, herbs, plants, soil, sage wands, water, blessed elements, vinegar, salt, sugar, milk, aloe, flowers, and your common weed.

It is up to you what you choose as your tools since they will appeal to you and you alone. When you have decided or gathered your tools, make sure to keep them wrapped and kept in a safe place. Caring for your tools and your altar are important facets in caring for your faith and your connection. So trust your energy and any visions you may receive about your path to help you.

Chapter 5: Spellwork

Finally, the chapter you've been waiting for, Spellwork. This chapter will only give you the basic types of spells you can use to help improve your life, protect yourself from negative forces, clearing yourself of negativity, banishing existing negative forces, and communing or meditative methods for visions.

Before You Cast.
It's important that I left this chapter last due to the overwhelming construct that Wicca is all about spells and symbols. Well, you'd be wrong. I would also deeply advise you to not believe what you see on television. Any faith has a mix of both the physical and spiritual realms. So while it may not be wrong to believe in miracles, it is wrong to believe that you can curse someone because you have to power to do it. Remember the Rede, the ardanes, and the Law of Three. These were mentioned in chapter 2 for a very good reason. If, as a solitary witch,

you decide your path is one where you teach yourself, then you must be extra careful and sure that you are not going to abuse the gift given to you. Spellcasting does not have Hollywood special effects behind it, it's subtle. It aligns with the forces that move the world and the universe. It is the same wavelength as the life force itself. To spell cast is to move that energy with your intention to have a result show itself. Be aware, in spellcasting, you are working with nature itself.

Spells normally use plant elements to assist. Spices like Corriander and Paprika have properties tied to making an herbal sachet that is used to help mend troubled relationships. Something like Peppermint might connect with you the most and therefore might be your go to plant when it comes to attaining your goals. Plants, even if they're simply weeds, can be used with oils for blessings, protections, or banishing. They can be used in edibles, sprays, soaps, or a simple pouch placed under your bed or pillow. Plants could also be turned into different teas. These teas can vary depending on the plant's purpose and if you're using a freshly picked version in its prime or youth, a dried version, or a powdered version. I recommend researching a book of plants to understand each property as they do have healing, blessing, cleansing, and banishing properties. Remember, a regular plant can have a multitude of uses based on how you use them.

Before every spell or ritual is a prayer for safety. This prayer needs to be able to protect you and your environment from being invaded by or attracting spirits or energies that do not belong there. A simple prayer is fine, but it must be said every time you decide to cast, meditate, or even ground yourself. When you place yourself in a position of spiritual vulnerability, you inadvertently open a way for other things to come in. So protect yourself by asking your deities to protect you as you do this.

Basic Spells.

Banishment Of Evil Deeds And Energy.

- Identify where the problem is and pray for protection as you anoint yourself with olive oil from head to toe.

- With your energy raised, use Sage, and Course Sea Salt as your tools.

- Invoke the aid of your deities and let them know what your intention is for the spell. In this case, you're banishing an evil from your home. Ask that their energy work through you and ask that they assist by capturing the energy when you identify where it is. Specify that you want them to take that energy back to where it came from and to seal the path so that none may come in as it leaves.

- If you have other spiritual aids, ask them to cleanse the house of other energies it may have left and to send them back as well.

- Always say this in the name of the creator.

- Proceed to cast out the evil with the salt as you say this. Make your way to your door as you toss the salt. Sage all areas in your home as you continue with your prayer. All corners and dark places must be touched by the sage. Work your way to your windows and doorway with the sage and sage the doorway itself.

- When you're finished, end your prayer as you would. Light an incense at your altar to thank the spirits for their help. Open the door or window to symbolize the spirits taking the evil away. When you feel this is done, you can close your window or doors.

- Ground yourself and send the extra energy into the earth. Thank it for all its work and help.

Casting Protection For Yourself.

- At your altar, raise your energy.

- Address your deities.

- Ask them for their protection. If there is something specific you want protection from, let them know.

- End the spell as a prayer in the way you would.

- Ground yourself.

Cleansing Oneself.

- Prepare a bath.

- Use tools you believe will clean your spirit. If you have flower oils, blessing oils, milk, mint, or sage then you can use those. If you have others you feel particularly strong with, then use those as well.

- Candles and incense help focus your intent with the deities and whom you want to help you.

- Ask for protection as you place your tools into the bath. Pray for what you wish to accomplish and where you want the bad energy to go. Let the spirits know, just like the Banishment spell, where you want them to take it and how you want to feel as a result of it leaving.

- Enter the bath. As you soak, submerge yourself completely in the water. If not, then douse yourself in the water beginning from the top of your head down to the bottoms of your feet while citing the prayer. Make sure you've raised your energy to do this.

- Continue to soak until you feel something leave. Say your prayer of thanks and end it as you would.

- Ground yourself.

Prayer For Good Fortune

- At your altar, say a prayer of protection.

- Address your deities. Let them know what your concerns are.

- Ask them not only for good fortune and good luck but for yourself to be guided and shown the way.

- Ask them for their continued support and thank them for everything they have done for you.

- End the prayer as you would.

Vision Work

- At your altar, say a prayer for protection.

- Address your deities.

- Dress in clothes you feel best represent pureness in a spiritual light.

- Go to a place where you commune. Take tools that help with meditation and represent your acceptance of your spiritual protection.

- Eyes can stay open or closed as you take deep breaths. You begin to feel relaxed as you drift somewhere else.

- There is no set time for this as seeing visions or signs come at their own time. What truly matters is the peace of mind you feel and have while doing this.

- Whether an epiphany or a visual sign, you have seen something. This is your answer. Smile and thank your deities as you would.

- Cleanse yourself in a regular bath or shower.

- Put your sacred clothes away.

- Ground yourself.

Conclusion

Thanks for making it through to the end of *Wicca For Beginners*, let's hope it was informative and able to provide you with all of the tools you need to achieve your goals whatever they may be.

The next step is to keep this book as a reference for all that you do in Wicca. Along with your teachings, you should be able to understand Wicca's foundation and it's varied history. So many intellects and papers have been written that helped Wicca onto its journey towards global acceptance, that it's important to always remember that it's not what you see on the silver screen or the small screen that makes your determination great, but the genuine knowledge one can glean from the wisdom of those who have passed on and those who are looking out for the future.

There are many things you can do now that you've finished this book, but the one thing you must always strive to be is yourself. Always learn more. Always be open and accepting of others. Always be aware of your surroundings. And always be aware of your needs and goals. This book was only the beginning for your road, so please keep it to remind yourself of those who came before and how they change the narrative on religion. So may you be blessed on your journey.

www.ingramcontent.com/pod-product-compliance
Lightning Source LLC
Chambersburg PA
CBHW071410080526
44587CB00017B/3235